Th
Abraham Lincoln

Kate Harvey

Rosen Classroom Books and Materials
New York

Published in 2002 by The Rosen Publishing Group, Inc.
29 East 21st Street, New York, NY 10010

Book Design: Ron A. Churley

Photo Credits: Cover, p. 1 © The Image Works Archive; pp. 5, 7, 9 © Corbis-Bettmann; p. 11 © PhotoWorld Inc./FPG International; pp. 13, 14 © Archive Photo.

ISBN: 0-8239-8211-4
6-pack ISBN: 0-8239-8614-4

Manufactured in the United States of America

Contents

Abraham Lincoln was the sixteenth president of the United States. He was known as a fair and **honest** man who believed in equal rights for all people.

Abe was born on a farm in Kentucky on February 12, 1809. He worked long hours every day helping his father with **chores**. Abe was able to go to school for a few months every year.

In 1816, Abe and his family moved to a small log cabin house in Indiana.

The first book Abe owned was about the life of George Washington.

Honest Abe

When Abe was twenty-one, he moved to Illinois. He worked many different jobs. One of his first jobs was splitting logs into rails for fences. He also worked as a store clerk.

Lincoln was often called "Honest Abe" for the fair way he dealt with people. One story says that Abe once walked several miles to give a woman change she had forgotten when she was at the store.

Abe's strength and skill with an ax earned him the nickname "Rail-splitter."

Many people liked Abe's kind way with people. He was **elected** to help make **decisions** for the Illinois state government at the age of twenty-five. He studied on his own to become a **lawyer**. Sometimes he walked as far as twenty miles to borrow books to study.

Abe worked as a lawyer for ten years before serving as a member of **Congress**.

Abe met many people as he traveled around practicing law.

9

In 1859, there was a big **disagreement** in the United States about **slavery**. The Southern states believed in slavery and the Northern states did not. Some Southern states wanted to leave the United States and become their own country.

Many people believed that as president, Lincoln could end slavery and keep the United States together. He was elected president on November 6, 1860.

Lincoln said, "A country cannot last if it is half slave and half free."

10

11

The Civil War

The disagreements between the North and South resulted in the **American Civil War** which began in 1861. In 1863, Lincoln gave a famous speech and signed a special paper that would lead to the freedom of slaves after the war ended. This special paper is called the Emancipation (ih-man-suh-PAY-shun) Proclamation (prah-kluh-MAY-shun). The war ended in 1865, and the Southern states remained part of the United States.

Abraham Lincoln ended slavery and kept the United States together as one country.

PROCLAMATION OF EMANCIPATION

13

After the war, many people were angry at Lincoln for ending slavery.

John Wilkes Booth, a very angry man who believed in slavery, shot President Lincoln. People in America were sad to lose such a great president. Abraham Lincoln is still remembered today for ending slavery and keeping the United States together.

Glossary

American Civil War   A war between the Northern and Southern states of the United States that lasted from 1861 to 1865.

chore   A job that has to be done often.

Congress   A branch of the United States government that makes laws for the whole country.

decision   A choice or judgment about something.

disagreement   When two people or groups have two different ways of thinking about something.

elect   To choose someone for public office by voting for him or her.

honest   Truthful.

lawyer   Someone who has studied law and acts for other people in a court of law.

slavery   The unfair system of being "owned" and having to work for someone else.

15

Index